His Divine Grace
A.C. Bhaktivedanta Swami Prabhupāda
Founder-Ācārya of the International Society for Krishna Consciousness

**Plate 1** "As a boat on water is swept away by a strong wind, even one of the senses on which the mind focuses can carry away a man's intelligence." *(p. 6)*

**Plate 2** "If the *yogī* is curious to know what the moon is like, he can transfer himself there, or if he is interested in higher planets, he can transfer himself there, just as travellers go to New York, Canada, or other cities on the Earth." *(p. 20)*

**Plate 3** "This whole material universe is like a small, insignificant cloud in the vast spiritual sky. It is encased by the *mahat-tattva*, matter. As a cloud has a beginning and an end, this material nature also has a beginning and an end. When the clouds disappear and the sky clears, we see everything as it is." *(p. 37)*

**Plate 4** "At the end of the day of Brahmā, all the lower planetary systems are covered with water, and the beings on them are annihilated. After this devastation and after the night of Brahmā passes, in the morning when Brahmā arises there is again creation and all these beings come forth. Thus subjection to creation and destruction is the nature of the material world." *(p. 35)*

**Plate 5** "To establish ourselves on the pure spiritual platform, we must take up the method of Kṛṣṇa consciousness. The gift of Caitanya Mahāprabhu, the chanting of the names of Kṛṣṇa—Hare Kṛṣṇa, Hare Kṛṣṇa, Kṛṣṇa Kṛṣṇa, Hare Hare/ Hare Rāma, Hare Rāma, Rāma Rāma, Hare Hare—facilitates this process. This method is called *bhakti-yoga* or *mantra-yoga*, and it is employed by the highest transcendentalists." *(pp. 12-13)*

**Plate 6** "We all want Kṛṣṇa and are hankering after Him. Kṛṣṇa is the most attractive, the most beautiful, the most opulent, the most powerful, and the most learned. That is the object of our hankering. We're hankering after the beautiful, the powerful, the learned, the wealthy. Kṛṣṇa is the reservoir of all of this. So we only need to turn our attention to Him and we will get everything—whatever we want." *(p. 29)*

**Plate 7** "The purpose of all Vedic instructions is to achieve the ultimate goal of life—to go back to Godhead. All scriptures from all countries aim at this goal. This has been the message of all religious reformers or *ācāryas*. No one advises us to make our permanent settlement here in the material world. All indications for the satisfaction of our soul's innermost desires point to those words of Kṛṣṇa beyond birth and death." *(pp. 55-56)*

# IS THERE LIFE AFTER DEATH?

India's most renowned Vedic authority presents startling evidence of the soul's incredible journey after death.

His Divine Grace A.C. Bhaktivedanta Swami Prabhupāda tells how the soul travels from body to body, and how we can end the cycle of birth and death by reaching the ultimate abode.

# BOOKS by

His Divine Grace

## A.C. Bhaktivedanta Swami Prabhupāda

published by Krishna Books Inc

Bhagavad-gītā As It Is

Śrīmad Bhāgavatam, First Canto

Kṛṣṇa, the Supreme Personality of Godhead

Śrī Īśopaniṣad

The Nectar of Devotion

The Nectar of Instruction

Teachings of Lord Chaitanya

Teachings of Queen Kuntī

The Science of Self-Realization

Rāja-vidyā: The King of Knowledge

Easy Journey to Other Planets

Kṛṣṇa, the Reservoir of Pleasure

The Perfection of Yoga

Beyond Birth and Death

On Chanting Hare Krishna

# BEYOND
# BIRTH & DEATH

His Divine Grace
A.C. Bhaktivedanta Swami Prabhupāda
Founder-*Ācārya* of the International Society for Krishna Consciousness

# *Beyond Birth and Death*

Contains the text and art originally published
by ISKCON Press in 1970.

Krishna Books Inc is licensed by the
Bhaktivedanta Book Trust
to print and publish the literary works of
**His Divine Grace**
**A.C. Bhaktivedanta Swami Prabhupāda**

Readers interested in obtaining other titles by the author
may contact Krishna Books Inc:

www.krishnabooks.org
or email: info@krishnabooks.org

**Krishna Books Inc**
578 Washington Blvd. Suite 808
Marina del Rey, CA 90292 USA



Library of Congress Catalog Card number: 72-84844
1970 English Edition
ISBN: 978-1-60293-004-9



KBI Reprints 2006-2013

Printed and bound by Thomson Press (India) Ltd.

# Contents

# 1

# We Are Not These Bodies

*dehī nityam avadhyo 'yaṁ*
*dehe sarvasya bhārata*
*tasmāt sarvāṇi bhūtāni*
*na tvaṁ śocitum arhasi*

"O descendant of Bharata, he who dwells in the body is eternal and can never be slain. Therefore you need not grieve for any creature." (*Bhagavad-gītā* 2.30)

The very first step in self-realization is realizing one's identity as separate from the body. "I am not this body but am spirit soul" is an essential realization for anyone who wants to transcend death and enter into the spiritual world beyond. It is not simply a matter of saying "I am not this body," but of actually realizing it. This is not as simple as it may seem at first. Although we are not these bodies but are pure consciousness, somehow or other we have become encased within the bodily dress. If we actually want the happiness and independence that transcend death, we have to establish ourselves and remain in our constitutional position as pure consciousness.

Living in the bodily conception, our idea of happiness is like that of a man in delirium. Some philosophers claim that this delirious condition of bodily identification should be cured by abstaining from all action. Because these material activities have been a source of distress for us, they claim that we should actually stop these activities. Their culmination of perfection is in a kind of Buddhistic *nirvāṇa*, in which no activities are performed. Buddha maintained that due to a combination of material elements, this body has come into existence, and that somehow or other if these material elements are separated or dismantled, the cause of suffering is removed. If the tax collectors give us too much difficulty because we happen to possess a large house, one simple solution is to destroy the house. However, *Bhagavad-gītā* indicates that this material body is not all in all. Beyond this combination of material elements, there is spirit, and the symptom of that spirit is consciousness.

Consciousness cannot be denied. A body without consciousness is a dead body. As soon as consciousness is removed from the body, the mouth will not speak, the eye will not see, nor the ears hear. A child can understand that. It is a fact that consciousness is absolutely necessary for the animation of the body. What is this consciousness? Just as heat or smoke are symptoms of fire, so consciousness is the symptom of the soul. The energy of the soul, or self, is produced in the shape of consciousness. Indeed, consciousness proves that the soul is present. This is not only the philosophy of *Bhagavad-gītā* but the conclusion of all Vedic literature.

The impersonalist followers of Śaṅkarācārya, as well as the Vaiṣṇavas following in the disciplic succession from Lord Śrī Kṛṣṇa, acknowledge the factual existence of the soul, but the Buddhist philosophers do not. The Buddhists contend that at a certain stage the combination of matter produces consciousness, but this argument is refuted by the fact that although we may have all the constituents of matter at our disposal, we cannot produce consciousness from them. All the material elements may be present in a dead man, but we cannot revive that man to consciousness. This body is not like a machine. When a part of a machine breaks down, it can be replaced, and the machine will work again, but when the body breaks down and consciousness leaves the body, there is no possibility of our replacing the broken part and rejuvenating the consciousness. The soul is different from the body, and as long as the soul is there, the body is animate. But there is no possibility of making the body animate in the absence of the soul.

Because we cannot perceive the soul by our gross senses, we deny it. Actually there are so many things that are there which we cannot see. We cannot see air, radio waves, or sound, nor can we perceive minute bacteria with our blunt senses, but this does not mean they are not there. By the aid of the microscope and other instruments, many things can be perceived which had previously been denied by the imperfect senses. Just because the soul, which is atomic in size, has not been perceived yet by senses or instruments, we should not conclude that it is not there. It can, however, be perceived by its symptoms and effects.

In *Bhagavad-gītā* Śrī Kṛṣṇa points out that all of our miseries are due to false identification with the body.

*mātrā-sparśās tu kaunteya*
*śītoṣṇa-sukha-duḥkha-dāḥ*
*āgamāpāyino 'nityās*
*tāṁs titikṣasva bhārata*

"O son of Kuntī, the nonpermanent appearance of heat and cold, happiness and distress, and their disappearance in due course, are like the appearance and disappearance of winter and summer seasons. They arise from sense perception, O scion of Bharata, and one must learn to tolerate them without being disturbed." (*Bg*. 2.14) In the summertime we may feel pleasure from contact with water, but in the winter we may shun that very water because it is too cold. In either case, the water is the same, but we perceive it as pleasant or painful due to its contact with the body.

All feelings of distress and happiness are due to the body. Under certain conditions the body and mind feel happiness and distress. Factually we are hankering after happiness, for the soul's constitutional position is that of happiness. The soul is part and parcel of the Supreme Being, who is *sac-cid-ānanda-vigrahaḥ*—the embodiment of knowledge, bliss, and eternity. Indeed, the very name *Kṛṣṇa*, which is nonsectarian, means "the greatest pleasure." *Kṛṣ* means "greatest," and *ṇa* means "pleasure." Kṛṣṇa is the epitome of pleasure, and being part and parcel of Him, we hanker for pleasure. A drop of ocean water has all the properties of the ocean itself, and we, although minute particles of the Supreme Whole, have the same energetic properties as the Supreme.

The atomic soul, although so small, is moving the entire body to act in so many wonderful ways. In the world we see so many cities, highways, bridges, great buildings, monuments, and great civilizations, but who has done all this? It is all done by the minute spirit spark within the body. If such wonderful things can be performed by the minute spirit spark, we cannot begin to imagine what can be accomplished by the Supreme Spirit Whole. The natural hankering of the minute spirit spark is for the qualities of the whole—knowledge, bliss, and eternality—but these hankerings are being frustrated due to the material body. The information on how to attain the soul's desire is given in *Bhagavad-gītā*.

At present we are trying to attain eternity, bliss, and knowledge by means of an imperfect instrument. Actually, our progress toward these goals is being blocked by the material body; therefore we have to come to the realization of our existence beyond the body. Theoretical knowledge that we are not these bodies will not do. We have to keep ourselves always separate as masters of the body, not as servants. If we know how to drive a car well, it will give us good service; but if we do not know how, we will be in danger.

The body is composed of senses, and the senses are always hungry after their objects. The eyes see a beautiful person and tell us, "Oh, there is a beautiful girl, a beautiful boy. Let's go see." The ears are telling us, "Oh, there is very nice music. Let us go hear it." The tongue is saying, "Oh, there is a very nice restaurant with palatable dishes. Let us go." In this way the senses are dragging us from one place to another, and because of this we are perplexed.

*indriyāṇāṁ hi caratāṁ*
*yan mano 'nuvidhīyate*
*tad asya harati prajñāṁ*
*vāyur nāvam ivāmbhasi*

"As a boat on the water is swept away by a strong wind, even one of the senses on which the mind focuses can carry away a man's intelligence." (*Bg.* 2.67)

It is imperative that we learn how to control the senses. The name *gosvāmī* is given to someone who has learned how to master the senses. *Go* means "senses," and *svāmī* means "controller"; so one who can control the senses is to be considered a *gosvāmī*. Kṛṣṇa indicates that one who identifies with the illusory material body cannot establish himself in his proper identity as spirit soul. Bodily pleasure is flickering and intoxicating, and we cannot actually enjoy it, because of its momentary nature. Actual pleasure is of the soul, not the body. We have to mold our lives in such a way that we will not be diverted by bodily pleasure. If somehow we are diverted, it is not possible for us to establish our consciousness in its true identity beyond the body.

*bhogaiśvarya-prasaktānāṁ*
*tayāpahṛta-cetasām*
*vyavasāyātmikā buddhiḥ*
*samādhau na vidhīyate*

*traiguṇya-viṣayā vedā*
*nistraiguṇyo bhavārjuna*
*nirdvandvo nitya-sattva-stho*
*niryoga-kṣema ātmavān*

"In the minds of those who are too attached to sense enjoyment and material opulence, and who are bewildered by such things, the resolute determination for devotional service to the Supreme Lord does not take place. The *Vedas* deal with the subject of the three modes of material nature. Rise above these modes, O Arjuna. Be transcendental to all of them. Be free from all dualities and from all anxieties for gain and safety, and be established in the Self." (*Bg.* 2.44-45)

The word *veda* means "book of knowledge." There are many books of knowledge, which vary according to the country, population, environment, etc. In India the books of knowledge are referred to as the *Vedas*. In the West they are called the Old Testament and New Testament. The Muhammadans accept the Koran. What is the purpose for all these books of knowledge? They are to train us to understand our position as pure soul. Their purpose is to restrict bodily activities by certain rules and regulations, and these rules and regulations are known as codes of morality. The Bible, for instance, has ten commandments intended to regulate our lives. The body must be controlled in order for us to reach the highest perfection, and without regulative principles, it is not possible to perfect our lives. The regulative principles may differ from country to country or from scripture to scripture, but that doesn't matter, for they are made according to the time and circumstances and the mentality of the people. But the principle of regulated control is the same. Similarly, the government sets down certain regulations to be obeyed by its citizens. There is no possibility of making advancement in government or civilization without some regulations. In the previous verse, Śrī Kṛṣṇa tells Arjuna that the regulative principles of the *Vedas* are meant to control the three modes of material nature—goodness, passion, and ignorance (*traiguṇya-viṣayā vedāḥ*). However, Kṛṣṇa is advising Arjuna to establish himself in his pure constitutional position as spirit soul, beyond the dualities of material nature.

As we have already pointed out, these dualities—such as heat and cold, pleasure and pain—arise due to the contact of the senses with their objects. In other words, they are born of identification with the body. Kṛṣṇa indicates that those who are devoted to enjoyment and power are carried away by the words of the *Vedas*, which promise heavenly enjoyment by sacrifice and regulated activity. Enjoyment is our birthright, for it is the characteristic of the spirit soul, but the spirit soul tries to enjoy materially, and this is the mistake.

Everyone is turning to material subjects for enjoyment and is compiling as much knowledge as possible. Someone is becoming a chemist, physicist, politician, artist, or whatever. Everyone knows something of everything or everything of something, and this is generally known as knowledge. But as soon as we leave the body, all of this knowledge is vanquished. In a previous life one may have been a great man of knowledge, but in this life he has to start again by going to school and learning how to read and write from the beginning. Whatever knowledge was acquired in the previous life is forgotten. The situation is that we are actually seeking eternal knowledge, but this cannot be acquired by this material body. We are all seeking enjoyment through these bodies, but bodily enjoyment is not our actual enjoyment. It is artificial. We have to understand that if we want to continue in this artificial enjoyment, we will not be able to attain our position of eternal enjoyment.

The body must be considered a diseased condition. A diseased man cannot enjoy himself properly; a man with jaundice, for instance, will taste sugar candy as bitter, but a healthy man can taste its sweetness. In either case, the sugar candy is the same, but according to our condition it tastes different. Unless we are cured of this diseased conception of bodily life, we cannot taste the sweetness of spiritual life. Indeed, it will taste bitter to us. At the same time, by increasing our enjoyment of material life, we are further complicating our diseased condition. A typhoid patient cannot eat solid food, and if someone gives it to him to enjoy, and he eats it, he is further complicating his malady and is endangering his life. If we really want freedom from the miseries of material existence, we must minimize our bodily demands and pleasures.

Actually, material enjoyment is not enjoyment at all. Real enjoyment does not cease. In the *Mahābhārata* there is a verse—*ramante yogino 'nante*—to the effect that the *yogīs* (*yogino*), those who are endeavoring to elevate themselves to the spiritual platform, are actually enjoying (*ramante*), but their enjoyment is anante, endless. This is because their enjoyment is in relation to the supreme enjoyer (Rāma), Śrī Kṛṣṇa. Bhagavān Śrī Kṛṣṇa is the real enjoyer, and *Bhagavad-gītā* (5.29) confirms this:

*bhoktāraṁ yajña-tapasāṁ*
*sarva-loka-maheśvaram*
*suhṛdaṁ sarva-bhūtānāṁ*
*jñātvā māṁ śāntim ṛcchati*

"The sages, knowing Me as the ultimate enjoyer of all sacrifices and austerities, the Supreme Lord of all planets and demigods, and the benefactor and well-wisher of all living entities, attain peace from the pangs of material miseries." *Bhoga* means "enjoyment," and our enjoyment comes from understanding our position as the enjoyed. The real enjoyer is the Supreme Lord, and we are enjoyed by Him.

An example of this relationship can be found in the material world between the husband and the wife: the husband is the enjoyer (*puruṣa*), and the wife is the enjoyed (*prakṛti*). The word *pri* means "woman." *Puruṣa*, or spirit, is the subject, and *prakṛti*, or nature, is the object. The enjoyment, however, is participated in both by the husband and the wife. When actual enjoyment is there, there is no distinction that the husband is enjoying more or the wife is enjoying less. Although the male is the predominator and the female is the predominated, there is no division when it comes to enjoyment. On a larger scale, no living entity is the enjoyer.

God expanded into many, and we constitute those expansions. God is one without a second, but He willed to become many in order to enjoy. We have experience that there is little or no enjoyment in sitting alone in a room talking to oneself. However, if there are five people present, our enjoyment is enhanced, and if we can discuss Kṛṣṇa before many, many people, the enjoyment is all the greater. Enjoyment means variety. God became many for His enjoyment, and thus our position is that of the enjoyed. That is our constitutional position and the purpose for our creation. Both enjoyer and enjoyed have consciousness, but the consciousness of the enjoyed is subordinate to the consciousness of the enjoyer. Although Kṛṣṇa is the enjoyer and we the enjoyed, the enjoyment can be participated in equally by everyone. Our enjoyment can be perfected when we participate in the enjoyment of God. There is no possibility of our enjoying separately on the bodily platform. Material enjoyment on the gross bodily platform is discouraged throughout *Bhagavad-gītā.*

*mātrā-sparśās tu kaunteya*
*śītoṣṇa-sukha-duḥkha-dāḥ*
*āgamāpāyino 'nityās*
*tāṁs titikṣasva bhārata*

"O son of Kuntī, the nonpermanent appearance of heat and cold, happiness and distress, and their disappearance in due course, are like the appearance and disappearance of winter and summer seasons.

They arise from sense perception, O scion of Bharata, and one must learn to tolerate them without being disturbed." (*Bg.* 2.14)

The gross material body is a result of the interaction of the modes of material nature, and it is doomed to destruction.

*antavanta ime dehā*
*nityasyoktāḥ śarīriṇaḥ*
*anāśino 'prameyasya*
*tasmād yudhyasva bhārata*

"Only the material body of the indestructible, immeasurable, and eternal living entity is subject to destruction; therefore, fight, O descendant of Bharata." (*Bg.* 2.18) Śrī Kṛṣṇa therefore encourages us to transcend the bodily conception of existence and attain to our actual spiritual life.

*guṇān etān atītya trīn*
*dehī deha-samudbhavān*
*janma-mṛtyu jarā-duḥkhair*
*vimukto 'mṛtam aśnute*

"When the embodied being is able to transcend these three modes [goodness, passion, and ignorance], he can become free from birth, death, old age, and their distresses and can enjoy nectar even in this life." (Bg. 14.20)

To establish ourselves on the pure *brahma-bhūta* spiritual platform, above the three modes, we must take up the method of Kṛṣṇa consciousness. The gift of Caitanya Mahāprabhu, the chanting of the names of

Kṛṣṇa—Hare Kṛṣṇa, Hare Kṛṣṇa, Kṛṣṇa Kṛṣṇa, Hare Hare/ Hare Rāma, Hare Rāma, Rāma Rāma, Hare Hare—facilitates this process. This method is called *bhakti-yoga* or *mantra-yoga*, and it is employed by the highest transcendentalists. How the transcendentalists realize their identity beyond birth and death, beyond the material body, and transfer themselves from the material universe to the spiritual universes are the subjects of the following chapters.

# 2
# Elevation at Death

There are different kinds of transcendentalists who are called *yogīs—haṭha-yogīs, jñāna-yogīs, dhyāna-yogīs*, and *bhakti-yogīs*—and all of them are eligible to be transferred to the spiritual world. The word *yoga* means "to link up," and the *yoga* systems are meant to enable us to link with the transcendental world. As mentioned in the previous chapter, originally we are all connected to the Supreme Lord, but now we have been affected by material contamination. The process is that we have to return to the spiritual world, and that process of linking up is called *yoga*. Another meaning of the word *yoga* is "plus." At the present moment we are minus God, or minus the Supreme. When we add Kṛṣṇa—or God—to our lives, this human form of life becomes perfect.

At the time of death we have to finish that process of perfection. During our lifetime we have to practice the method of approaching that perfection so that at the time of death, when we have to give up this material body, that perfection can be realized.

*prayāṇa-kāle manasācalena*
*bhaktyā yukto yoga-balena caiva*

*bhruvor madhye prāṇam āveśya samyak*
*sa taṁ paraṁ puruṣam upaiti divyam*

"One who, at the time of death, fixes his life air between the eyebrows and in full devotion engages himself in remembering the Supreme Lord, will certainly attain to the Supreme Personality of Godhead." (*Bg.* 8.10)

Just as a student studies a subject for four or five years and then takes his examination and receives a degree, similarly, with the subject of life, if we practice during our lives for the examination at the time of death, and if we pass the examination, we are transferred to the spiritual world. Our whole life is examined at the time of death.

*yaṁ yaṁ vāpi smaran bhāvaṁ*
*tyajaty ante kalevaram*
*taṁ tam evaiti kaunteya*
*sadā tad-bhāva-bhāvitaḥ*

"Whatever state of being one remembers when he quits his body, that state he will attain without fail." (*Bg.* 8.6)

There is a Bengali proverb that says that whatever one does for perfection will be tested at the time of his death. In *Bhagavad-gītā* Kṛṣṇa describes what one should do when giving up the body. For the *dhyāna-yogī* (meditator) Śrī Kṛṣṇa speaks the following verses:

*yad akṣaraṁ veda-vido vadanti*
*viśanti yad yatayo vīta-rāgāḥ*

*yad icchanto brahmacaryaṁ caranti*
*tat te padaṁ saṅgraheṇa pravakṣye*

*sarva-dvārāṇi saṁyamya*
*mano hṛdi nirudhya ca*
*mūrdhny ādhāyātmanaḥ prāṇam*
*āsthito yoga-dhāraṇām*

"Persons learned in the *Vedas*, who utter *oṁkāra* and who are great sages in the renounced order, enter into Brahman. Desiring such perfection, one practices celibacy. I shall now explain to you this process by which one may attain salvation. The yogic situation is that of detachment from all sensual engagements. Closing all the doors of the senses and fixing the mind on the heart and the life air at the top of the head, one establishes himself in *yoga*." (*Bg*. 8.11-12)

In the yoga system this process is called *pratyāhāra*, which means "just the opposite." Although during life the eyes are engaged in seeing worldly beauty, at death one has to retract the senses from their objects and see the beauty within. Similarly, the ears are accustomed to hearing so many sounds in the world, but at the moment of death one has to hear the transcendental *oṁkāra* from within.

*oṁ ity ekākṣaraṁ brahma*
*vyāharan mām anusmaran*
*yaḥ prayāti tyajan dehaṁ*
*sa yāti paramāṁ gatim*

"After being situated in this *yoga* practice and vibrating the sacred syllable *oṁ*, the supreme combination of letters, if one thinks of the Supreme Personality of Godhead and quits his body, he will certainly reach the spiritual planets." (*Bg.* 8.13) In this way, all the senses have to be stopped in their external activities and concentrated on the form of *viṣṇu-mūrti*, the form of God. The mind is very turbulent, but it has to be fixed on the Lord in the heart. When the mind is fixed within the heart and the life air is transferred to the top of the head, one can attain perfection of *yoga*.

At this point the *yogī* determines where he is to go. In the material universe there are innumerable planets, and beyond this universe there is the spiritual universe. The *yogīs* have information of these places from Vedic literatures. Just as one going to America can get some idea what the country is like by reading books, one can also have knowledge of the spiritual planets by reading Vedic literatures. The *yogī* knows all these descriptions, and he can transfer himself to any planet he likes, without the help of spaceships. Space travel by mechanical means is not the accepted process for elevation to other planets. Perhaps with a great deal of time, effort, and money a few men may be able to reach other planets by material means—spaceships, space suits, etc.—but this is a very cumbersome and impractical method. In any case, it is not possible to go beyond the material universe by mechanical means.

The generally accepted method for transferral to higher planets is the practice of the meditational *yoga* system or *jñāna* system. The *bhakti-yoga* system, however, is not to be practiced for transferral to any material planet, for those who are servants of Kṛṣṇa, the Supreme Lord, are not interested in any planets in this material world because they know that on whatever planet one enters in the material sky, the four principles of birth, old age, disease, and death are present. On higher planets, the duration of life may be longer than on this earth, but death is there nonetheless. By "material universe" we refer to those planets where birth, old age, disease, and death reside, and by "spiritual universe" we refer to those planets where there is no birth, old age, disease, and death. Those who are intelligent do not try to elevate themselves to any planet within the material universe.

If one tries to enter higher planets by mechanical means, instant death is assured, for the body cannot stand the radical changes in atmosphere. But if one attempts to go to higher planets by means of the *yoga* system, he will acquire a suitable body for entrance. We can see this demonstrated on this earth, for we know it is not possible for us to live in the sea, in a watery atmosphere, nor is it possible for aquatics to live on the earth. As we understand that even on this planet one has to have a particular type of body to live in a particular place, so a particular type of body is required for other planets. On the higher planets, bodies live much longer than on earth, for six months on earth is equal to one day on the higher planets. Thus the *Vedas* describe that those who live on higher planets live upwards of ten thousand earth years. Yet despite such a long life span, death awaits everyone. Even if one lives twenty thousand or fifty thousand or even millions of years, in the material world the years are all counted, and death is there. How can we escape this subjugation by death? That is the lesson of *Bhagavad-gītā*.

*na jāyate mriyate vā kadācin*
*nāyaṁ bhūtvā bhavitā vā na bhūyaḥ*
*ajo nityaḥ śāśvato 'yaṁ purāṇo*
*na hanyate hanyamāne śarīre*

"For the soul there is never birth nor death. Nor, once having been, does he ever cease to be. He is unborn, eternal, ever-existing, undying, and primeval. He is not slain when the body is slain." (*Bg.* 2.20)

We are spirit soul, and as such we are eternal. Why, then, should we subject ourselves to birth and death? One who asks this question is to be considered intelligent. Those who are Kṛṣṇa conscious are very intelligent, because they are not interested in gaining entrance to any planet where there is death. They will reject a long duration of life in order to attain a body like God's. *Īśvaraḥ paramaḥ kṛṣṇaḥ sac-cid-ānanda-vigrahaḥ. Sat* means "eternal," *cit* means "full of knowledge," and *ānanda* means "full of pleasure." Kṛṣṇa is the reservoir of all pleasure. If we transfer ourselves from this body into the spiritual world—either to Kṛṣṇaloka (Kṛṣṇa's planet) or any other spiritual planet—we will receive a similar *sac-cid-ānanda* body. Thus the aim of those who are in Kṛṣṇa consciousness is different from those who are trying to promote themselves to higher planets within this material world.

The self, or soul, of the individual is a minute spiritual spark. The perfection of *yoga* lies in the transferral of this spiritual spark to the top of the head. Having attained this, the *yogī* can transfer himself to any planet in the material world, according to his desire. If the *yogī* is curious to know what the moon is like, he can transfer himself there, or if he is interested in higher planets, he can transfer himself there, just as travelers go to New York, Canada, or other cities on the earth. Wherever one goes on earth, he finds the same visa and customs systems operating, and on all the material planets one can similarly see the principles of birth, old age, disease, and death operating.

*Oṁ ity ekākṣaraṁ brahma*: at the point of death the *yogī* can pronounce *oṁ*, *oṁkāra*, the concise form of transcendental sound vibration. If the *yogī* can vibrate this sound and at the same time remember Kṛṣṇa, or Viṣṇu (*mām anusmaran*), he attains the highest goal. It is the process of yoga to concentrate the mind on Viṣṇu. The impersonalists imagine some form of the Supreme Lord, but the personalists do not imagine this; they actually see. Whether one imagines Him or actually sees Him, one has to concentrate his mind on the personal form of Kṛṣṇa.

*ananya-cetāḥ satataṁ*
*yo māṁ smarati nityaśaḥ*
*tasyāhaṁ sulabhaḥ pārtha*
*nitya-yuktasya yoginaḥ*

"For one who remembers Me without deviation, I am easy to obtain, O son of Pṛthā, because of his constant engagement in devotional service." (*Bg.* 8.14)

Those who are satisfied with temporary life, temporary pleasure, and temporary facilities are not to be considered intelligent, at least not according to *Bhagavad-gītā*. According to the *Gītā*, one whose brain substance is very small is interested in temporary things. We are eternal, so why should we be interested in temporary things? No one wants a nonpermanent situation. If we are living in an apartment and the landlord asks us to vacate, we are sorry, but we are not sorry if we move into a better apartment. It is our nature, because we are permanent, to want permanent residence. We don't wish to die, because in actuality we are permanent. Nor do we want to grow old or be diseased, because these are all external or nonpermanent states. Although we are not meant to suffer from fever, sometimes fever comes, and we have to take precautions and remedies to get well again. The fourfold miseries are like a fever, and they are all due to the material body. If somehow we can get out of the material body, we can escape the miseries that are integral with it.

For the impersonalists to get out of this temporary body, Kṛṣṇa here advises that they vibrate the syllable *oṁ*. In this way they can be assured of transmigration into the spiritual world. However, although they may enter the spiritual world, they cannot enter into any of the planets there. They remain outside, in the *brahmajyoti*. The *brahmajyoti* may be compared to the sunshine, and the spiritual planets may be compared to the sun itself. In the spiritual sky the impersonalists remain in the effulgence of the Supreme Lord, the *brahmajyoti*. The impersonalists are placed in the *brahmajyoti* as spiritual sparks, and in this way the *brahmajyoti* is filled with spiritual sparks. This is what is meant by merging into the spiritual existence.

It should not be considered that one merges into the *brahmajyoti* in the sense of becoming one with it; the individuality of the spiritual spark is retained, but because the impersonalist does not want to take a personal form, he is found as a spiritual spark in that effulgence. Just as the sunshine is composed of so many atomic particles, so the *brahmajyoti* is composed of so many spiritual sparks.

However, as living entities we want enjoyment. Being, in itself, is not enough. We want bliss (*ānanda*) as well as being (*sat*). In his entirety, the living entity is composed of three qualities—eternality, knowledge, and bliss. Those who enter impersonally into the *brahmajyoti* can remain there for some time in full knowledge that they are now merged homogeneously with Brahman, but they cannot have that eternal *ānanda*, bliss, because that part is wanting. One may remain alone in a room for some time and may enjoy himself by reading a book or engaging in some thought, but it is not possible to remain in that room for years and years at a time, and certainly not for all eternity. Therefore, for one who merges impersonally into the existence of the Supreme, there is every chance of falling down again into the material world in order to acquire some association. This is the verdict of *Śrīmad-Bhāgavatam*. Astronauts may travel thousands and thousands of miles, but if they do not find rest on some planet, they have to return again to earth. In any case, rest is required. In the impersonal form, rest is uncertain. Therefore *Śrīmad-Bhāgavatam* says that even after so much endeavor, if the impersonalist enters into the spiritual world and acquires an impersonal form, he returns again into the material world because of neglecting to serve the Supreme Lord in love and devotion. As long as we are here on earth, we must learn to practice to love and serve Kṛṣṇa, the Supreme Lord. If we learn this, we can enter into those spiritual planets. The impersonalist's position in the spiritual world is nonpermanent, for out of loneliness he will attempt to acquire some association. Because he does not associate personally with the Supreme Lord, he has to return again to the world and associate with conditioned living entities there.

It is of utmost importance, therefore, that we know the nature of our constitutional position: we want eternity, complete knowledge, and also pleasure. When we are left alone for a long time in the impersonal *brahmajyoti*, we cannot have pleasure, and therefore we accept the pleasure given by the material world. But in Kṛṣṇa consciousness, real pleasure is enjoyed. In the material world it is generally accepted that the highest pleasure is sex. This is a perverted reflection of the sex pleasure in the spiritual world, the pleasure of association with Kṛṣṇa. But we should not think that the pleasure there is like the sex pleasure in the material world. No, it is different. But unless sex life is there in the spiritual world, it cannot be reflected here. Here it is simply a perverted reflection, but the actual life is there in Kṛṣṇa, who is full of all pleasure. Therefore, the best process is to train ourselves now, so that at the time of death we may transfer ourselves to the spiritual universe, to Kṛṣṇaloka, and there associate with Kṛṣṇa. In *Brahma-saṁhitā* (5.29) Śrī Kṛṣṇa and His abode are described thus:

*cintāmaṇi-prakara-sadmasu kalpa-vṛkṣa-*
*lakṣāvṛteṣu surabhīr abhipālayantam*
*lakṣmī-sahasra-śata-sambhrama-sevyamānaṁ*
*govindam ādi-puruṣaṁ tam ahaṁ bhajāmi*

"I worship Govinda, the primeval Lord, the first progenitor, who is tending the cows, fulfilling all desire, in abodes built with spiritual gems, surrounded by millions of wish-fulfilling trees, always served with great reverence and affection by hundreds and thousands of *lakṣmīs*, or *gopīs*." This is a description of Kṛṣṇaloka. The houses are made of what is called "touchstone." Whatever touchstone touches immediately turns into gold. The trees are wish-fulfilling trees, or "desire trees," for one can receive from them whatever he wishes. In this world we get mangoes from mango trees and apples from apple trees, but there from any tree one can get whatever he desires. Similarly, the cows are called *surabhi*, and they yield an endless supply of milk. These are descriptions of the spiritual planets found in Vedic scriptures.

In this material world we have become acclimatized to birth, death, and all sorts of suffering. Material scientists have discovered many facilities for sense enjoyment and destruction, but they have discovered no solution to the problems of old age, disease, and death. They cannot make any machine that will check death, old age, or disease. We can manufacture something that will accelerate death, but nothing that will stop death. Those who are intelligent, however, are not concerned with the fourfold miseries of material life, but with elevation to the spiritual planets. One who is continuously in trance (*nitya-yuktasya yoginaḥ*) does not divert his attention to anything else. He is always situated in trance. His mind is always filled with the thought of Kṛṣṇa, without deviation (*ananya-cetāḥ satatam*). *Satatam* refers to anywhere and any time.

In India I lived in Vṛndāvana, and now I am in America, but this does not mean that I am out of Vṛndāvana, because if I think of Kṛṣṇa always, then I'm always in Vṛndāvana, regardless of the material designation. Kṛṣṇa consciousness means that one always lives with Kṛṣṇa on that spiritual planet, Goloka Vṛndāvana, and that one is simply waiting to give up this material body. *Smarati nityaśaḥ* means "continuously remembering," and for one who is continuously remembering Kṛṣṇa, the Lord becomes *tasyāhaṁ sulabhaḥ*—easily purchased. Kṛṣṇa Himself says that He is easily purchased by this *bhakti-yoga* process. Then why should we take to any other process? We can chant Hare Kṛṣṇa, Hare Kṛṣṇa, Kṛṣṇa Kṛṣṇa, Hare Hare/ Hare Rāma, Hare Rāma, Rāma Rāma, Hare Hare twenty-four hours daily. There are no rules and regulations. One can chant in the street, in the subway, or at his home or office. There is no tax and no expense. So why not take to it?

# 3

# Liberation from Material Planets

The *jñānīs* and *yogīs* are generally impersonalists, and although they attain the temporary form of liberation by merging into the impersonal effulgence, the spiritual sky, according to *Śrīmad-Bhāgavatam* their knowledge is not considered pure. By penances, austerities, and meditations they can rise up to the platform of the Supreme Absolute, but as has been explained, they again fall down to the material world, because they have not taken Kṛṣṇa's personal features seriously. Unless one worships the lotus feet of Kṛṣṇa, he again has to descend to the material platform. The ideal attitude should be, "I am Your eternal servitor. Please let me somehow engage in Your service." Kṛṣṇa is called *ajitaḥ*—unconquerable—for no one can conquer God, but according to *Śrīmad-Bhāgavatam*, one with this attitude easily conquers the Supreme. *Śrīmad-Bhāgavatam* also recommends that we give up this futile process to measure the Supreme. We cannot even measure the limitations of space, what to speak of the Supreme. It is not possible to measure the length and breadth of Kṛṣṇa by one's minuscule knowledge, and one who arrives at this conclusion is considered intelligent by Vedic literature. One should come to understand, submissively, that he is a very insignificant segment of the universe. Abandoning the endeavor to understand the Supreme by limited knowledge or mental speculation, we should become submissive and hear of the Supreme through the authoritative sources such as *Bhagavad-gītā* or through the lips of a realized soul.

In Bhagavad-gītā Arjuna is hearing about God from the lips of Śrī Kṛṣṇa Himself. In this way Arjuna set the criterion for understanding the Supreme by submissive hearing. It is our position to hear *Bhagavad-gītā* from the lips of Arjuna or his bona fide representative, the spiritual master. After hearing, it is necessary to practice this acquired knowledge in daily life. "My dear Lord, You are unconquerable," the devotee prays, "but by this process, by hearing, You are conquered." God is unconquerable, but He is conquered by the devotee who abandons mental speculation and listens to authoritative sources.

According to *Brahma-saṁhitā* there are two ways of acquiring knowledge—the ascending process and the descending process. By the ascending process one is elevated by knowledge acquired by himself. In this way one thinks, "I don't care for any authorities or books. I will attain knowledge myself by meditation, philosophy, etc. In this way I will understand God." The other process, the descending process, involves receiving knowledge from higher authorities. *Brahma-saṁhitā* states that if one takes to the ascending process and travels at the speed of mind and wind for millions of years, he will still end up not knowing. For him, the subject matter will remain elusive and inconceivable. But that subject matter is given in

*Bhagavad-gītā*: *ananya-cetāḥ*. Kṛṣṇa says to meditate on Him without deviation from the path of devotional service in submission. For one who worships Him in this way—*tasyāhaṁ sulabhaḥ*: "I become easily available." This is the process: if one works for Kṛṣṇa twenty-four hours a day, Kṛṣṇa cannot forget him. By becoming submissive, he can attract the attention of God. As Guru Mahārāja Bḥaktisiddhānta Sarasvatī used to say, "Don't try to see God. Is God to come and stand before us like a servant just because we want to see Him? That is not the submissive way. We have to oblige Him by our love and service."

The proper process for approaching Kṛṣṇa was given to humanity by Lord Caitanya Mahāprabhu, and Rūpa Gosvāmī, His first disciple, appreciated it. Rūpa Gosvāmī was a minister in the Muhammadan government, but he left the government to become a disciple of Caitanya Mahāprabhu. When he first went to see the Lord, Rūpa Gosvāmī approached Him with the following verse:

*namo mahā-vadānyāya*
*kṛṣṇa-prema-pradāya te*
*kṛṣṇāya kṛṣṇa-caitanya-*
*nāmne gaura-tviṣe namaḥ*

"I offer my respectful obeisances unto the Supreme Lord, Śrī Kṛṣṇa Caitanya, who is more magnanimous than any other *avatāra*, even Kṛṣṇa Himself, because He is bestowing freely what no one else has ever given—pure love of Kṛṣṇa." Rūpa Gosvāmī called Caitanya Mahāprabhu "the most munificent, the most charitable personality," because He was offering the most precious thing of all very cheaply—love of God. We all want Kṛṣṇa and are all hankering after Him. Kṛṣṇa is the most attractive, the most beautiful, the most opulent, the most powerful, and the most learned. That is the object of our hankering. We're hankering after the beautiful, the powerful, the learned, the wealthy. Kṛṣṇa is the reservoir of all of this, so we need only turn our attention toward Him, and we will get everything. Everything—whatever we want. Whatever is our heart's desire will be fulfilled by this process of Kṛṣṇa consciousness.

For one who dies in Kṛṣṇa consciousness, as stated before, entrance into Kṛṣṇaloka, the supreme abode where Kṛṣṇa resides, is guaranteed. At this point one may ask what the advantage is in going to that planet, and Kṛṣṇa Himself answers:

*mām upetya punar janma*
*duḥkhālayam aśāśvatam*
*nāpnuvanti mahātmānaḥ*
*saṁsiddhiṁ paramāṁ gatāḥ*

"After attaining Me, the great souls, who are yogīs in devotion, never return to this temporary world, which is full of miseries, because they have attained the highest perfection." (*Bg.* 8.15)

This material world is certified by Śrī Kṛṣṇa, the creator, as *duḥkhālayam*—full of miseries. How then can we make it comfortable? Is it possible to make this world comfortable by the so-called advancement of science? No, this is not possible. As a result, we do not even wish to know what these miseries are. The miseries, as stated before, are birth, old age, disease, and death, and because we cannot make a solution to them, we try to set them aside. Science has no power to solve these miseries that are always giving us trouble. Instead, they divert our attention to the making of spaceships or atomic bombs. The solution to these problems is given here in *Bhagavad-gītā*: if one attains to Kṛṣṇa's platform he does not have to return again to this earth of birth and death. We should try to understand that this place is full of miseries. It takes a certain amount of developed consciousness to understand this. Cats and dogs and hogs cannot understand that they are suffering. Man is called a rational animal, but his rationality is being used to further his animalistic propensities instead of to find out how to get liberation from this miserable condition. Here Kṛṣṇa explicitly states that one who comes to Him will never be reborn to suffer miseries again. Those great souls who come to Him have attained the highest perfection of life, which alleviates the living entity from the suffering of conditional existence.

One of the differences between Kṛṣṇa and an ordinary being is that an ordinary entity can be in only one place at a time, but Kṛṣṇa can be everywhere in the universe and yet also in His own abode, simultaneously. Kṛṣṇa's abode in the transcendental kingdom is called Goloka Vṛndāvana. The Vṛndāvana in India is that same Vṛndāvana descended on this earth. When Kṛṣṇa descends Himself by His own internal potency, His *dhāma*, or abode, also descends. In other words, when Kṛṣṇa descends on this earth, He manifests Himself in that particular land. Despite this, Kṛṣṇa's abode remains eternally in the transcendental sphere, in the

Vaikuṇṭhas. In this verse Kṛṣṇa proclaims that one who comes to His abode in the Vaikuṇṭhas never has to take birth again in the material world. Such a person is called a *mahātmā*. The word *mahātmā* is generally heard in the West in connection with *Mahatma* Gandhi, but we should understand that *mahātmā* is not the title of a politician. Rather, *mahātmā* refers to the first-class Kṛṣṇa conscious man who is eligible to enter into the abode of Kṛṣṇa. The mahātmā's perfection is this: to utilize the human form of life and the resources of nature to extricate himself from the cycle of birth and death.

An intelligent person knows that he does not want miseries, but they are inflicted upon him by force. As stated before, we are always in a miserable condition due to this mind, body, natural disturbances, or other living entities. There is always some kind of misery inflicted upon us. This material world is meant for misery; unless the misery is there, we cannot come to Kṛṣṇa consciousness. Miseries are actually an impetus and help to elevate us to Kṛṣṇa consciousness. An intelligent man questions why these miseries are inflicted on him by force. However, modern civilization's attitude is, "Let me suffer. Let me cover it by some intoxication, that's all." But as soon as the intoxication is over, the miseries return. It is not possible to make a solution to the miseries of life by artificial intoxication. The solution is made by Kṛṣṇa consciousness.

One may point out that although the devotees of Kṛṣṇa are trying to enter Kṛṣṇa's planet, everyone else is interested in going to the moon. Isn't going to the moon also perfection? The tendency to travel to other planets is always present in the living entity. One name for the living entity is *sarva-gata*, which means "one who wants to travel everywhere." Travel is part of the nature of the living entity. The desire to go to the moon is not a new thing. The *yogīs* also are interested in entering the higher planets, but in *Bhagavad-gītā* (8.16) Kṛṣṇa points out that this will not be of any help.

*ābrahma-bhuvanāl lokāḥ*
*punar āvartino 'rjuna*
*mām upetya tu kaunteya*
*punar janma na vidyate*

"From the highest planet in the material world down to the lowest, all are places of misery wherein repeated birth and death take place. But one who attains to My abode, O son of Kuntī, never takes birth again." The universe is divided into higher, middle, and lower planetary systems. The earth is considered to be a member of the middle planetary system. Kṛṣṇa points out that even if one enters into the highest planet of all, called Brahmaloka, there is still repetition of birth and death. Other planets in the universe are full of living entities. We should not think that we are here and that all the other planets are vacant. From experience we can see that no place on earth is vacant of living entities. If we dig deep down into the earth, we find worms; if we go deep into the water, we find aquatics; if we go into the sky, we find so many birds. How is it possible to conclude that other planets have no living entities? But Kṛṣṇa points out that even if we enter into those planets where great demigods reside, we will still be subjected to death. Again, Kṛṣṇa repeats that upon reaching His planet, one need not take birth again.

We should be very serious about attaining our eternal life full of bliss and knowledge. We have forgotten that this is actually our aim of life, our real self-interest. Why have we forgotten? We have simply been entrapped by the material glitter, by skyscrapers, big factories, and political play, although we know that however big we build skyscrapers, we will not be able to live here indefinitely. We should not spoil our energy in building mighty industries and cities to further entrap ourselves in material nature; rather, our energy should be used to develop Kṛṣṇa consciousness, in order to attain a spiritual body whereby we may enter into Kṛṣṇa's planet. Kṛṣṇa consciousness is not a religious formula or some spiritual recreation; it is the most important part of the living entity.

# 4

# The Sky Beyond the Universe

If even the higher planets in this universe are subject to birth and death, why do great yogīs strive for elevation to them? Although they may have many mystic powers, these *yogīs* still have the tendency to want to enjoy the facilities of material life. On the higher planets, it is possible to live for incredibly long lifetimes. The time calculation on these planets is indicated by Śrī Kṛṣṇa:

*sahasra-yuga-paryantam*
*ahar yad brahmaṇo viduḥ*
*rātriṁ yuga-sahasrāntāṁ*
*te 'ho-rātra-vido janāḥ*

"By human calculation, a thousand ages taken together is the duration of Brahmā's one day. And such also is the duration of his night." (*Bg.* 8.17)

One *yuga* covers 4,300,000 years. This number multiplied by one thousand is calculated to be twelve hours of Brahmā on the planet Brahmaloka. Similarly, another twelve-hour period covers the night. Thirty such days equal a month, twelve months a year, and Brahmā lives for one hundred such years. Life on such a planet is indeed long, yet even after trillions of years, the inhabitants of Brahmaloka have to face death. Unless we go to the spiritual planets, there is no escape from death.

*avyaktād vyaktayaḥ sarvāḥ*
*prabhavanty ahar-āgame*
*rātry-āgame pralīyante*
*tatraivāvyakta-saṁjñake*

"When Brahmā's day is manifest, this multitude of living entities comes into being, and at the arrival of Brahmā's night, they are all annihilated." (*Bg.* 8.18) At the end of the day of Brahmā, all the lower planetary systems are covered with water, and the beings on them are annihilated. After this devastation and after the night of Brahmā passes, in the morning when Brahmā arises there is again creation, and all these beings come forth. Thus subjection to creation and destruction is the nature of the material world.

*bhūta-grāmaḥ sa evāyaṁ*
*bhūtvā bhūtvā pralīyate*
*rātry-āgame 'vaśaḥ pārtha*
*prabhavaty ahar-āgame*

"Again and again the day comes, and this host of beings is active; and again the night falls, O Pārtha, and they are helplessly dissolved." (*Bg.* 8.19) Although the living entities do not like devastation, that devastation will come and overflood the planets until all living beings on the planets stay merged in water throughout the night of Brahmā. But as day comes, the water gradually disappears.

*paras tasmāt tu bhāvo 'nyo*
*'vyakto 'vyaktāt sanātanaḥ*
*yaḥ sa sarveṣu bhūteṣu*
*naśyatsu na vinaśyati*

"Yet there is another nature, which is eternal and is transcendental to this manifested and unmanifested matter. It is supreme and is never annihilated. When all in this world is annihilated, that part remains as it is." (*Bg.* 8.20) We cannot calculate the extent of the material universe, but we have Vedic information that there are millions of universes within the entire creation, and beyond these material universes there is another sky, which is spiritual. There all the planets are eternal, and the lives of all the beings on them are eternal. In this verse the word *bhāvaḥ* means "nature," and here another nature is indicated. In this world we have experience also of two natures. The living entity is spirit, and as long as he is within matter, matter is moving, and as soon as the living entity, the spiritual spark, is out of the body, the body is immovable. The spiritual nature is called Kṛṣṇa's superior nature, and the material is called the inferior. Beyond this material nature there is a superior nature, which is totally spiritual. It is not possible to understand this by experimental knowledge. We can see millions and millions of stars through a telescope, but we cannot approach them. We have to understand our incapabilities. If we cannot understand the material universe by experimental knowledge, what is the possibility of understanding God and His kingdom? It is not possible experimentally. We have to understand by hearing *Bhagavad-gītā*. We cannot understand who our father is by experimental knowledge; we have to hear the word of our mother and believe her. If we do not believe her, there is no way of knowing. Similarly, if we just stick to the Kṛṣṇa conscious method, all information about Kṛṣṇa and His kingdom will be revealed.

*Paras tu bhāvaḥ* means "superior nature," and vyaktaḥ refers to what we see manifested. We can see that the material universe is manifested through the earth, sun, stars, and planets. And beyond this universe is another nature, an eternal nature. *Avyaktāt sanātanaḥ.* This material nature has a beginning and an end, but that spiritual nature is *sanātanaḥ*—eternal. It has neither beginning nor end. How is this possible? A cloud may pass over the sky, and it may appear to cover a great distance, but actually it is only a small speck covering an insignificant part of the whole sky. Because we are so small, if only a few hundred miles is covered by cloud, it appears that the whole sky is covered. Similarly, this whole material universe is like a small, insignificant cloud in the vast spiritual sky. It is encased by the *mahat-tattva*, matter. As a cloud has a beginning and an end, this material nature also has a beginning and an end. When the clouds disappear and the sky clears, we see everything as it is. Similarly, the body is like a cloud passing over the spirit soul. It stays for some time, gives some by-products, dwindles, and then vanishes. Any kind of material phenomenon that we observe is subject to these six transformations of material nature—it comes into being, grows, stays for a while, produces some by-products, dwindles, and then vanishes. Kṛṣṇa indicates that beyond this changing, cloudlike nature there is a spiritual nature, which is eternal. In addition, when this material nature is annihilated, that *avyaktāt sanātanaḥ* will remain.

In Vedic literatures there is a good deal of information about the material and spiritual skies. In the Second Canto of *Śrīmad-Bhāgavatam* there are descriptions of the spiritual sky and of its inhabitants. There is even information given that there are spiritual airplanes in the spiritual sky and that the liberated entities there travel about on these planes like lightning. Everything that we find here can also be found there in reality. Here in the material sky everything is an imitation, or shadow, of that which exists in the spiritual sky. As in a cinema we simply see a show or facsimile of the real thing, in *Śrīmad-Bhāgavatam* it is said that this material world is but a combination of matter modeled after the reality, just as a mannequin of a girl in a store window is modeled after a girl. Every sane man knows that the mannequin is an imitation. Śrīdhara Svāmī says that because the spiritual world is real, this material world, which is an imitation, *appears* to be real. We must understand the meaning of reality—reality means existence which cannot be vanquished; reality means eternity.

*nāsato vidyate bhāvo*
*nābhāvo vidyate sataḥ*
*ubhayor api dṛṣṭo 'ntas*
*tv anayos tattva-darśibhiḥ*

"Those who are seers of the truth have concluded that of the nonexistent there is no endurance, and of the existent there is no cessation. This seers have concluded by studying the nature of both." (*Bg.* 2.16)

Real pleasure is Kṛṣṇa, whereas material pleasure, which is temporary, is not actual. Those who can see things as they are do not take part in shadow pleasure. The real aim of human life is to attain to the spiritual sky, but as *Śrīmad-Bhāgavatam* points out, most people do not know about it. Human life is meant to understand reality and to be transferred into it. All Vedic literature instructs us not to remain in this darkness. The nature of this material world is darkness, but the spiritual world is full of light and yet is not illumined by fire or electricity. Kṛṣṇa hints of this in the Fifteenth Chapter of *Bhagavad-gītā* (15.6):

*na tad bhāsayate sūryo*
*na śaśāṅko na pāvakaḥ*
*yad gatvā na nivartante*
*tad dhāma paramaṁ mama*

"That abode of Mine is not illumined by the sun or moon, nor by electricity. One who reaches it never returns to this material world."

The spiritual world is called unmanifested because it cannot be perceived by material senses.

*avyakto 'kṣara ity uktas*
*tam āhuḥ paramāṁ gatim*
*yaṁ prāpya na nivartante*
*tad dhāma paramaṁ mama*

"That supreme abode is called unmanifested and infallible, and it is the supreme destination. When one goes there, he never comes back. That is My supreme abode." (*Bg.* 8.21) A great journey is indicated in this verse. We have to be able to penetrate outer space, traverse the material universe, penetrate its covering, and enter the spiritual sky. *Paramāṁ gatim*—that journey is supreme. There is no question of going a few thousand miles away from this planet and then returning. This sort of journey is not very heroic. We have to penetrate the whole material universe. This we cannot do by spaceships but by Kṛṣṇa consciousness. One who is absorbed in Kṛṣṇa consciousness and who at the time of death thinks of Kṛṣṇa is at once transferred there. If we at all want to go to that spiritual sky and cultivate eternal, blissful life, full of knowledge, we will have to begin now to cultivate a *sac-cid-ānanda* body. It is said that Kṛṣṇa has a *sac-cid-ānanda* body—*īśvaraḥ paramaḥ kṛṣṇaḥ sac-cid-ānanda-vigrahaḥ*—and we also have a similar body of eternity, knowledge, and bliss, but it is very small and is covered by the dress of matter. If somehow or other we are able to give up this false dress, we can reach that spiritual kingdom. If once we can attain that spiritual world, return is not necessary (*yaṁ prāpya na nivartante*).

Everyone, then, should try to go to that *dhāma paramam*—Kṛṣṇa's supreme abode. Kṛṣṇa Himself comes to call us, and He gives us literatures as guidebooks and sends His bona fide representatives. We should take advantage of this facility given to human life. For one who reaches that supreme abode, penances, austerities, yogic meditations, and so on are no longer required, and for one who does not reach it, all penances and austerities are a useless waste of time. The human form of life is an opportunity to get this boon, and it is the duty of the state, parents, teachers, and guardians to elevate those who have acquired this human form of life to attain this perfection of life. Simply eating, sleeping, mating, and quarreling like cats and dogs is not civilization. We should properly utilize this human form of life and take advantage of this knowledge to prepare ourselves in Kṛṣṇa consciousness, so that twenty-four hours of the day we will be absorbed in Kṛṣṇa and at death at once transfer to that spiritual sky.

*puruṣaḥ sa paraḥ pārtha*
*bhaktyā labhyas tv ananyayā*
*yasyāntaḥ-sthāni bhūtāni*
*yena sarvam idaṁ tatam*

"The Supreme Personality of Godhead, who is greater than all, is attainable by unalloyed devotion. Although He is present in His abode, He is all-pervading, and everything is situated within Him." (*Bg.* 8.22)

If we are at all interested in reaching that supreme abode, the process, as indicated here, is *bhakti*. *Bhaktyā* means devotional service, submission to the Supreme Lord. The root word for *bhaktyā* is *bhaj*, which means "service." The definition of *bhakti* given in the *Nārada-pañcarātra* is "freedom from designation." If one is determined to get out of all the designations that are attached to the pure spirit soul, and which arise due to the body and are always changed when the body is changed, one can attain to *bhakti. Bhakti* is realizing that one is pure spirit and not matter at all. Our real identity is not this body, which is simply a covering of the spirit, but our real identity is *dāsa*, servant of Kṛṣṇa. When one is situated in his real identity and is rendering service to Kṛṣṇa, he is a *bhakta. Hṛṣīkeṇa hṛṣīkeśa-sevanam*: when our senses are free from material designations, we will utilize them in the service of the master of the senses, Hṛṣīkeśa, or Kṛṣṇa.

As Rūpa Gosvāmī points out, we have to serve Kṛṣṇa favorably. Generally we want to serve God for some material purpose or gain. Of course, one who goes to God for material gain is better than one who never goes, but we should be free from desire for material benefit. Our aim should be to understand Kṛṣṇa. Of course Kṛṣṇa is unlimited, and it is not possible to understand Him, but we have to accept what we can understand. *Bhagavad-gītā* is specifically presented for our understanding. Through receiving knowledge in this way, we should know that Kṛṣṇa is pleased, and we should serve Him favorably, according to His pleasure. Kṛṣṇa consciousness is a great science with immense literatures, and we should utilize them for the attainment of *bhakti*.

*Puruṣaḥ sa paraḥ*: in the spiritual sky, the Supreme Lord is present as the Supreme Person. There are innumerable self-luminous planets there, and in each one an expansion of Kṛṣṇa resides. They are four-armed and have innumerable names. They are all persons—they are not impersonal. These *puruṣas*, or persons, can be approached by *bhakti*, not by challenge, philosophical speculation, or mental concoctions, nor by physical exercises, but by devotion without the deviations of fruitive activity.

What is the *puruṣaḥ*, the Supreme Person, like? *Yasyāntaḥ-sthāni bhūtāni yena sarvam idaṁ tatam*: every living entity and everything is within Him, and yet He is without, all-pervading. How is that? He is just like the sun, which is situated in one place and yet is present all over by its rays. Although God is situated in His *dhāma paramam*, His energies are distributed everywhere. Nor is He different from His energies, inasmuch as the sunshine and the sun are nondifferent. Since Kṛṣṇa and His energies are nondifferent, we can see Kṛṣṇa everywhere if we are advanced in devotional service.

*premāñjana-cchurita-bhakti-vilocanena*
*santaḥ sadaiva hṛdayeṣu vilokayanti*

"I worship the original Personality of Godhead, Govinda, whom the pure devotees whose eyes are smeared with the ointment of love of Godhead always observe within their hearts." (*Brahma-saṁhitā* 5.38)

Those who are filled with love of God see God constantly before them. It is not that we saw God last night and He is no longer present. No. For one who is Kṛṣṇa conscious, Kṛṣṇa is always present and can be perceived constantly. We simply have to develop the eyes to see Him.

Due to our material bondage, the covering of the material senses, we cannot understand what is spiritual. But this ignorance can be removed by this process of chanting Hare Kṛṣṇa. How is this? A sleeping man may be awakened by sound vibration.

Although a man may be for all intents and purposes unconscious—he cannot see, feel, smell, etc.—the sense of hearing is so prominent that a sleeping man may be awakened just by sound vibration. Similarly, the spirit soul, although now overpowered by the sleep of material contact, can be revived by this transcendental sound vibration of Hare Kṛṣṇa, Hare Kṛṣṇa, Kṛṣṇa Kṛṣṇa, Hare Hare/ Hare Rāma, Hare Rāma, Rāma Rāma, Hare Hare. Hare Kṛṣṇa is simply an address to the Supreme Lord and His energies. *Hare* means energy, and *Kṛṣṇa* is the name of the Supreme Lord, so when we chant Hare Kṛṣṇa we are saying, "O energy of the Lord, O Lord, please accept me." We have no other prayer for acceptance by the Lord. There is no question of praying for daily bread, for the bread is always there. Hare Kṛṣṇa is but an address to the Supreme Lord, requesting Him to accept us. Lord Caitanya Mahāprabhu Himself prayed,

*ayi nanda-tanuja kiṅkaraṁ*
*patitaṁ māṁ viṣame bhavāmbudhau*
*kṛpayā tava pāda-paṅkaja-*
*sthita-dhūlī-sadṛśaṁ vicintaya*

"O son of Mahārāja Nanda, I am Your eternal servitor, and although I am so, somehow or other I have fallen in the ocean of birth and death. Please, therefore, pick me up from this ocean of death and fix me as one of the atoms at Your lotus feet." (*Śikṣāṣṭaka* 5) The only hope for a man fallen in the middle of the ocean is that someone will come and pick him up. If someone just comes and hauls him but a few feet out of the water, he is immediately relieved. Similarly, if we are somehow lifted from the ocean of birth and death by the process of Kṛṣṇa consciousness, we are immediately relieved.

Although we cannot perceive the transcendental nature of the Supreme Lord, His name, fame, and activities, if we establish ourselves in Kṛṣṇa consciousness, gradually God will reveal Himself before us. We cannot see God by our own endeavor, but if we qualify ourselves, God will reveal Himself, and then we will see. No one can order God to come before him and dance, but we do have to work in such a way that Kṛṣṇa will be pleased to reveal Himself to us.

Kṛṣṇa gives us information about Himself in *Bhagavad-gītā*, and there is no question of doubting it; we just have to feel it, understand it. There is no preliminary qualification necessary for the understanding of *Bhagavad-gītā*, because it is spoken from the absolute platform. The simple process of chanting the names of Kṛṣṇa will reveal what one is, what God is, what the material and spiritual universes are, why we are conditioned, how we can get out of that conditioning—and everything else, step by step. Actually, the process of belief and revelation is not foreign to us. Every day we place faith in something that we have confidence will be revealed later. We may purchase a ticket to go to India, and on the basis of the ticket we have faith that we will be transported there. Why should we pay money for a ticket? We do not just give the money to anyone. The company is authorized and the airline is authorized, so faith is created. Without faith we cannot take one step forward in the ordinary course of our life. Faith we must have, but it must be faith in that which is authorized. It is not that we have blind faith, but that we accept something that is recognized. *Bhagavad-gītā* is recognized and accepted as scripture by all classes of men in India, and as far as outside India is concerned, many scholars, theologians, and philosophers accept *Bhagavad-gītā* as a great, authoritative work. There is no question that *Bhagavad-gītā* is authority. Even Professor Albert Einstein, such a scientist, read *Bhagavad-gītā* regularly.

From *Bhagavad-gītā* we have to accept that there is a spiritual universe which is the kingdom of God. If somehow we are transported to a country where we are informed that we will no longer have to undergo birth, old age, disease, and death, will we not be happy? If we heard of such a place, surely we would try as hard as possible to go there. No one wants to grow old; no one wants to die. Indeed, a place free of such sufferings would be our heart's desire. Why do we want this? Because we have the right, the prerogative, to want it. We are eternal, blissful, and full of knowledge, but having been covered by this material entanglement, we have forgotten ourselves. Therefore *Bhagavad-gītā* gives us the advantage of being able to revive our original status.

The Śaṅkarites and Buddhists claim that the world beyond is void, but *Bhagavad-gītā* does not disappoint us like this. The philosophy of voidness has simply created atheists. We are spiritual beings, and we want enjoyment, but as soon as our future is void, we will become inclined to enjoy this material life. In this way, the impersonalists discuss the philosophy of voidism while trying as much as possible to enjoy this material life. One may enjoy speculation in this way, but there is no spiritual benefit.

*brahma-bhūtaḥ prasannātmā*
*na śocati na kāṅkṣati*
*samaḥ sarveṣu bhūteṣu*
*mad-bhaktiṁ labhate parām*

"One who is thus transcendentally situated at once realizes the Supreme Brahman. He never laments or desires to have anything; he is equally disposed to every living entity. In that state he attains pure devotional service unto Me." (*Bg.* 18.54)

He who has progressed in devotional life and who is relishing service to Kṛṣṇa will automatically become detached from material enjoyment. The symptom of one absorbed in *bhakti* is that he is fully satisfied with Kṛṣṇa.

# 5

# Associating with Kṛṣṇa

If one gets something superior, he naturally gives up all inferior things. We want enjoyment, but impersonalism and voidism have created such an atmosphere that we have become addicted to material enjoyment. There must be enjoyment in connection with the Supreme Person (*puruṣaḥ sa paraḥ*), whom we can see face to face. In the spiritual sky we are able to speak personally with God, play with Him, eat with Him, etc. All of this can be attained by *bhaktyā*—transcendental loving service. However, this service must be without adulteration, that is to say, we must love God without expecting material remuneration. Loving God to become one with Him is also a form of adulteration.

One of the major differences between the spiritual sky and the material sky is that in the spiritual sky the head or leader of the spiritual planets has no rival. In all cases, the predominating personality in the spiritual planets is a plenary expansion of Śrī Kṛṣṇa. The Supreme Lord and His multifarious manifestations preside over all the Vaikuṇṭha planets. On earth, for instance, there is rivalry for the position of president or prime minister, but in the spiritual sky everyone acknowledges the Supreme Personality of Godhead to be supreme. Those who do not acknowledge Him and attempt to rival Him are placed into the material universe, which is just like a prison house. As in any city there is a prison, and the prison forms a very insignificant part of the whole city, so the material universe is a prison for the conditioned souls. It forms an insignificant part of the spiritual sky, but it is not outside the spiritual sky, just as a prison is not outside of the city.

The inhabitants of the Vaikuṇṭha planets in the spiritual sky are all liberated souls. In *Śrīmad-Bhāgavatam* we are informed that their bodily features are exactly like God's. On some of these planets God is manifested with two arms, and on others He has four. The inhabitants of these planets, like the Supreme Lord, also manifest two and four arms, and it is said that one cannot distinguish between them and the Supreme Person. In the spiritual world there are five kinds of liberation. *Sāyujya-mukti* is a form of liberation in which one merges into the impersonal existence of the Supreme Lord, called Brahman. Another form of liberation is *sārūpya-mukti*, by which one receives features exactly like God's. Another is *sālokya-mukti*, by which one can live in the same planet with God. By *sārṣṭi-mukti* one can have opulences similar to the Supreme Lord's. Another type enables one to remain always with God as one of His associates, just like Arjuna, who is always with Kṛṣṇa as His friend. One can have any of these five forms of liberation, but of the five the *sāyujya-mukti*, merging with the impersonal aspect, is not accepted by Vaiṣṇava devotees. A Vaiṣṇava wishes to worship God as He is and retain his separate individuality to serve Him, whereas the Māyāvādī impersonal philosopher wishes to lose his individuality and merge into the existence of the Supreme. This merging is recommended neither by Śrī Kṛṣṇa in *Bhagavad-gītā* nor by the disciplic succession of Vaiṣṇava philosophers. Lord Caitanya Mahāprabhu wrote on this subject in His *Śikṣāṣṭaka* (4):

*na dhanaṁ na janaṁ na sundarīṁ*
*kavitāṁ vā jagad-īśa kāmaye*
*mama janmani janmanīśvare*
*bhavatād bhaktir ahaitukī tvayi*

"O almighty Lord! I have no desire to accumulate wealth, nor have I any desire to enjoy beautiful women, nor do I want any number of followers. What I want only is that I may have Your causeless devotional service in my life, birth after birth." Here Lord Caitanya Mahāprabhu refers to "birth after birth." When there is birth after birth, there is no liberation. In liberation one either attains the spiritual planets or merges into the existence of the Supreme—in either case, there is no question of rebirth into the material world. But Caitanya Mahāprabhu doesn't care whether He is liberated or not: His only concern is to be engaged in Kṛṣṇa consciousness, to serve the Supreme Lord. The devotee doesn't care where he is, nor does he care whether he is born in the animal society, human society, demigod society, or whatever—he only prays to God that he not forget Him and that he always be able to engage in His transcendental service. These are symptoms of pure devotion. Of course a devotee, wherever he is, remains in the spiritual kingdom, even while in this material body. But he does not demand anything from God for his own personal elevation or comfort.

Although Śrī Kṛṣṇa indicates that He can be easily reached by one who is devoted to Him, there is an element of risk involved for the *yogīs* who practice other methods of *yoga*. For them, He has given directions in *Bhagavad-gītā* (8.23) regarding the proper time to leave the gross body.

*yatra kāle tv anāvṛttim*
*āvṛttiṁ caiva yoginaḥ*
*prayātā yānti taṁ kālaṁ*
*vakṣyāmi bharatarṣabha*

"O best of the Bhāratas, I shall now explain to you the different times at which, passing away from this world, one does or does not come back." Here Kṛṣṇa indicates that if one is able to leave his body at a particular time, he can become liberated, never to return to the material world. On the other hand, he indicates that if one dies at another time, he has to return. There is this element of chance, but there is no question of chance for a devotee always in Kṛṣṇa consciousness, for he is guaranteed entrance into the abode of Kṛṣṇa by dint of his devotion to the Lord.

*agnir jyotir ahaḥ śuklaḥ*
*ṣaṇ-māsā uttarāyaṇam*
*tatra prayātā gacchanti*
*brahma brahma-vido janāḥ*

"Those who know the Supreme Brahman pass away from the world during the influence of the fiery god, in the light, at an auspicious moment, during the fortnight of the moon and the six months when the sun travels in the north." (*Bg.* 8.24) The sun spends six months on the northern side of the equator and six months on the southern side. In *Śrīmad-Bhāgavatam* we have information that as the planets are moving, so also the sun is moving. If one dies when the sun is situated in the northern hemisphere, he attains liberation.

*dhūmo rātris tathā kṛṣṇaḥ*
*ṣaṇ-māsā dakṣiṇāyanam*
*tatra cāndramasaṁ jyotir*
*yogī prāpya nivartate*

*śukla-kṛṣṇe gatī hy ete*
*jagataḥ śāśvate mate*
*ekayā yāty anāvṛttim*
*anyayāvartate punaḥ*

"The mystic who passes away from this world during the smoke, the night, the moonless fortnight, or in the six months when the sun passes to the south, or who reaches the moon planet, again comes back. According to the *Vedas*, there are two ways of passing from this world—one in light and one in darkness. When one passes in light, he does not come back; but when one passes in darkness, he returns." (*Bg.* 8.25-26)

This is all by chance. We do not know when we are going to die, and we may die accidentally at any time. But for one who is a bhakti-yogī, who is established in

Kṛṣṇa consciousness, there is no question of chance. He is always sure.

*naite sṛtī pārtha jānan*
*yogī muhyati kaścana*
*tasmāt sarveṣu kāleṣu*
*yoga-yukto bhavārjuna*

"The devotees who know these two paths, O Arjuna, are never bewildered. Therefore, be always fixed in devotion." (*Bg*. 8.27)

It has already been ascertained that at the time of death, if one can think of Kṛṣṇa, he is immediately transferred to the abode of Kṛṣṇa.

*anta-kāle ca mām eva*
*smaran muktvā kalevaram*
*yaḥ prayāti sa mad-bhāvaṁ*
*yāti nāsty atra saṁśayaḥ*

*abhyāsa-yoga-yuktena*
*cetasā nānya-gāminā*
*paramaṁ puruṣaṁ divyaṁ*
*yāti pārthānucintayan*

"And whoever, at the time of death, quits his body remembering Me alone, at once attains My nature. Of this there is no doubt. He who meditates on the Supreme Personality of Godhead, his mind constantly engaged in remembering Me, undeviated from the path, he, O Pārtha [Arjuna], is sure to reach Me." (*Bg*. 8.5, 8.8) Such meditation on Kṛṣṇa may seem very difficult, but it is not. If one practices Kṛṣṇa consciousness by chanting the *mahā-mantra*, Hare Kṛṣṇa, Hare Kṛṣṇa, Kṛṣṇa Kṛṣṇa, Hare Hare/ Hare Rāma, Hare Rāma, Rāma Rāma, Hare Hare, he will be quickly helped. Kṛṣṇa and His name are nondifferent, and Kṛṣṇa and His transcendental abode are also nondifferent. By sound vibration we can have Kṛṣṇa associate with us. If, for instance, we chant Hare Kṛṣṇa on the street, we will see that Kṛṣṇa is going with us, just as when we look up and see the moon overhead, we perceive that it is also going with us. If Kṛṣṇa's inferior energy may appear to go with us, is it not possible for Kṛṣṇa Himself to be with us when we are chanting His names? He will keep us company, but we have to qualify to be in His company. If, however, we are always merged in the thought of Kṛṣṇa, we should rest assured that Kṛṣṇa is always with us. Lord Caitanya Mahāprabhu prays,

*nāmnām akāri bahudhā nija-sarva-śaktis*
*tatrārpitā niyamitaḥ smaraṇe na kālaḥ*
*etādṛśī tava kṛpā bhagavan mamāpi*
*durdaivam īdṛśam ihājani nānurāgaḥ*

"O my Lord! Your holy name alone can render all benediction upon the living beings, and therefore You have hundreds and millions of names, like *Kṛṣṇa* and *Govinda.* In these transcendental names You have invested all Your transcendental energies, and there is no hard and fast rule for chanting these holy names. O my Lord! You have so kindly made approach to You easy by Your holy names, but unfortunate as I am, I have no attraction for them." (*Śikṣāṣṭaka* 2)

Merely by chanting we can have all the advantages of personal association with Kṛṣṇa. Lord Caitanya Mahāprabhu, who is not only considered to be a realized soul but an incarnation of Kṛṣṇa Himself, has pointed out that in this age of Kali, although men have no real facilities for self-realization, Kṛṣṇa is so kind that He has given this *śabda* (sound incarnation) to be utilized as the *yuga-dharma*, or way of realization of this age. No special qualification is necessary for this method; we need not even know Sanskrit. The vibrations of Hare Kṛṣṇa are so potent that anyone can immediately begin chanting them, without any knowledge of Sanskrit whatsoever.

*vedeṣu yajñeṣu tapaḥsu caiva*
*dāneṣu yat puṇya-phalaṁ pradiṣṭam*
*atyeti tat sarvam idaṁ viditvā*
*yogī paraṁ sthānam upaiti cādyam*

"A person who accepts the path of devotional service is not bereft of the results derived from studying the Vedas, performing austere sacrifices, giving charity, or pursuing philosophical and fruitive activities. At the end he reaches the supreme abode." (*Bg.* 8.28)
Here Kṛṣṇa says that the purpose of all Vedic instructions is to achieve the ultimate goal of life—to go back to Godhead. All scriptures from all countries aim at this goal. This has also been the message of all religious reformers or *ācāryas.* In the West, for example, Lord Jesus Christ spread this same message. Similarly, Lord Buddha and Muhammad. No one advises us to make our permanent settlement here in

this material world. There may be small differences according to country, time, and circumstance, and according to scriptural injunction, but the main principle that we are not meant for this material world but for the spiritual world is accepted by all genuine transcendentalists. All indications for the satisfaction of our soul's innermost desires point to those worlds of Kṛṣṇa beyond birth and death.

# Keep in Touch...

If you would like a free information package and a catalogue of books available send your name and address in an email to:

**info@krishnabooks.org**

or mail the coupon below:

Name ______________________________

Address ____________________________

State ______________________ Zip ________

Country ____________________________

Email Address _______________________

Return this coupon to:

**Krishna Books Inc**
**578 Washington Blvd. Suite 808**
**Marina del Rey, CA 90292 USA**